Inspirational Quotes from some of the World's Greatest Minds

90 Quotes for 30 Days to Change Your Life

**WRITTEN BY
ALI POURNAMDARIAN**

Inquiry, the lantern in the dark,
Ignites the flame, a vital spark.
To question, ponder, seek the light,
And free the mind from endless night.

Cast off the shackles of routine,
Unveil the realms that lie unseen.
For in the depths of self-awareness,
Resides the seed of inner happiness.

Release the burdens that weigh you down,
Discover the treasures that lie around.
In self-reflection's gentle sound,
A symphony of growth can be found.

Embrace the whispers of your soul,
Let intuition guide you towards your goal.
Unleash the power that lies within,
Ignite the flames that yearn to begin.

Copyright © 2023 by Ali Pournamdarian
All rights reserved.

    No part of this publication may be reproduced, distributed, or transmitted in any form or by any means, including photocopying, recording, or other electronic or mechanical methods, without the prior written permission of the author. For permission requests, contact Myperspective@shaw.ca.

First edition 2023

Content

- Introduction 1
- Quotes from Eastern Philosophers and Scholars 4
  - Buddha 5
  - Confucius 6
  - Lao Tzu 7
  - Khwarizmi (Al-Khwarizmi) 8
  - Farabi (Al-Farabi) 9
  - Avicenna (Ibn Sina) 10
  - Ghazali (Al-Ghazali) 11
  - Dogen 12
  - Rumi (Jalaluddin Rumi/Molana) 13
  - Hafiz 14
  - Ibn Khaldun 15
  - Wang Yangming 16
  - Matsuo Basho 17
  - Rabindranath Tagore 18
  - Byung-Chul Han 19
- Quotes from Western Philosophers and Scholars 20
  - Socrates 21
  - Plato 22
  - Aristotle 23
  - Boethius 24
  - William Shakespeare 25
  - René Descartes 26
  - Isaac Newton 27
  - George Berkeley 28
  - Jean-Jacques Rousseau 29
  - Immanuel Kant 30
  - Hegel 31
  - Friedrich Nietzsche 32

- Albert Einstein 33
- Jean-Paul Sartre 34
- Quentin Meillassoux 35

The Power of Your Thoughts 36

Introduction

"If I have seen further than others, it is by standing upon the shoulders of giants."
Sir Isaac Newton

Human beings have always looked up to great thinkers and philosophers for guidance and inspiration. Through their wise words and teachings, they have helped people navigate through difficult times, find meaning in their lives, and strive toward a better future. Great thinkers and philosophers remind us of our humanity as they often focus on human limitations and our place in the world by asking us to question our assumptions and beliefs. They challenge us to think critically and to examine the world around us with a fresh perspective. By reading their words, we can expand our minds and develop new ways of thinking. We can find motivation and inspiration to pursue our own goals and dreams.

In this book, I have selected thirty of the greatest minds in human history from both Eastern and Western cultures in chronological order. Without a doubt, the choice of which philosophers and thinkers to name as "great" or "inspirational" is subjective and varies depending on individual perspectives and cultural backgrounds. There are countless philosophers and thinkers throughout history who have made significant contributions to human knowledge and understanding, and it can be difficult to choose just a few to highlight as particularly noteworthy.

That being said, certain philosophers and thinkers have had a particularly profound impact on human history and continue to influence our thinking today. For example, Socrates, Plato, and Aristotle are often regarded as the founding fathers of Western philosophy, and their ideas have influenced countless philosophers and thinkers throughout history. Similarly, figures such as Confucius, Buddha, and Lao Tzu have had a significant impact on Eastern philosophy and continue to be studied and revered today.

The choice of which philosophers and thinkers to highlight as "great" or "inspirational" may also depend on the context in which they are being discussed. For example, in a discussion of ethics, the names of figures such as Immanuel Kant and Friedrich Nietzsche may be highlighted, while in the field of science or mathematics, scientists such as Einstein, Khwarizmi, and Newton may come to mind. There are also many poets that we can highlight as "great thinkers" or "inspirational" philosophers. I have only mentioned a few names that I was familiar with them.

I tried to bring only three quotes from each of the selected philosophers and thinkers, and I separated these quotes into three groups: One to begin your day with motivation, a reminder during the day to keep you inspired, and a reflection at the end of the day. I think it would be a good practice to take some time before sleeping to think back on your day and consider the events, experiences, and emotions that you encountered throughout the day. This could involve contemplating your successes and failures, reviewing your goals and priorities, or simply taking a moment to be mindful and present. The goal of reflecting at the end of the day is to gain insight into yourself, your life, and your choices and to learn from your experiences to make positive changes or adjustments moving forward. It is a way to promote self-awareness, personal growth, and overall well-being.

    I have also provided a summary of the life and the philosophy or viewpoint of the scholars that I have selected for their quotes. I have made these summaries as concise as possible to have one page for each day of the month from one scholar. These summaries are also inspirational by themselves, and not only give the readers some historical context and help the readers to increase their cultural literacy, but they also help the readers to broaden their perspectives and to think critically. Without a doubt, these summaries can also enrich our intellectual lives, provide guidance, and foster personal growth.

    In conclusion, the inspirational words of great thinkers and philosophers are essential for our personal growth and development. They offer us guidance, wisdom, motivation, and hope and remind us of our shared humanity and the possibilities for positive change. By studying their ideas and teachings, we can expand our minds and live more fulfilling lives.

Quotes from Eastern Philosophers and Scholars

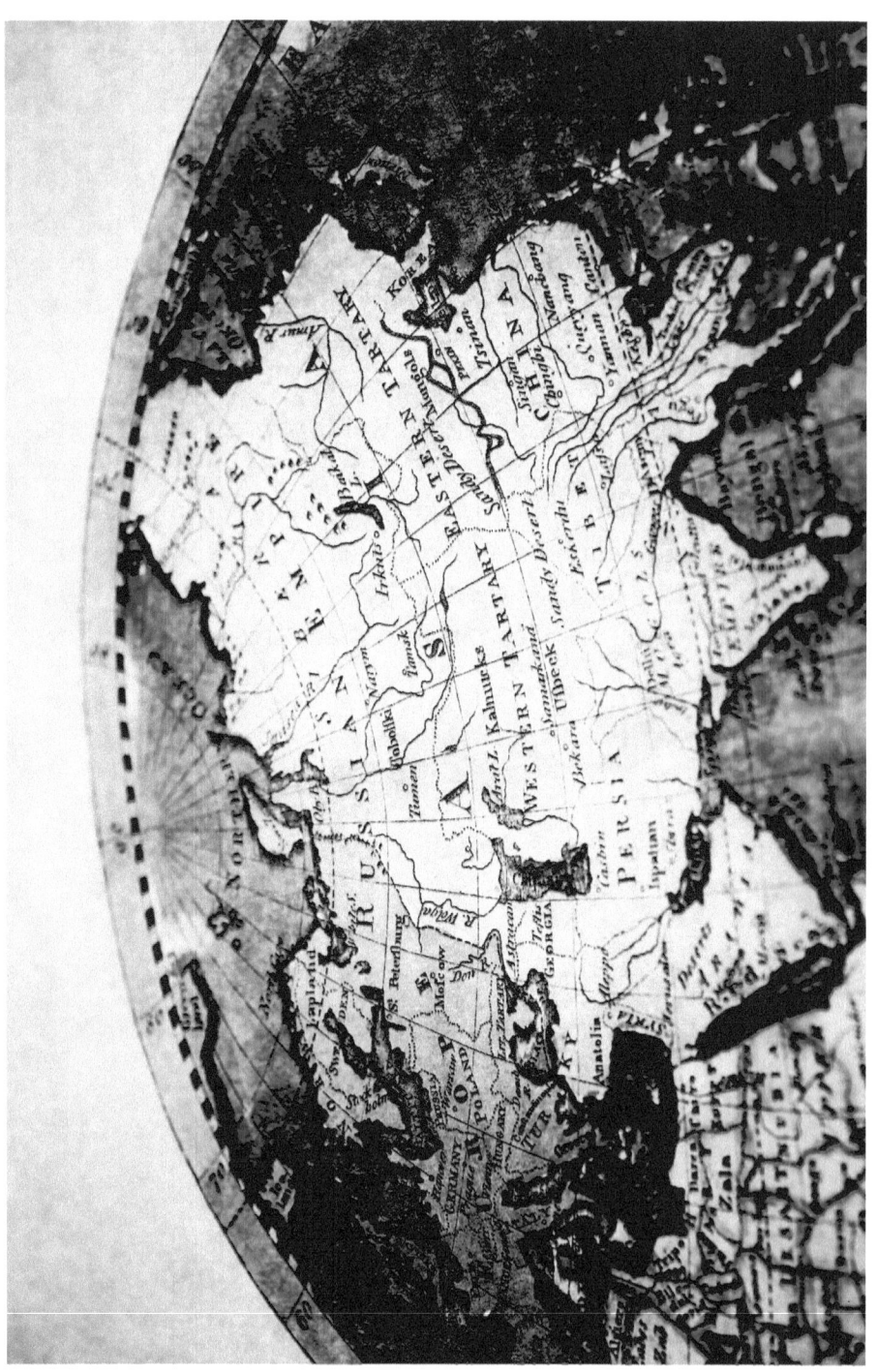

Buddha (563 BCE - 483 BCE) was an ancient Indian philosopher and spiritual leader. Buddha's philosophy is centered around the Four Noble Truths and the Eightfold Path. The Four Noble Truths state that suffering exists, suffering arises from attachment and desire, suffering can be ended, and the path to the end of suffering is the Eightfold Path that consists of right understanding, right intention, right speech, right action, right livelihood, right effort, right mindfulness, and right concentration.

Begin your day with this quote:

"The mind is everything. What you think you become."
Buddha

Remind yourself during the day:

"Thousands of candles can be lit from a single candle, and the life of the candle will not be shortened. Happiness never decreases by being shared."
Buddha

Read this quote and reflect at the end of the day:

"Do not dwell in the past, do not dream of the future, concentrate the mind on the present moment."
Buddha

Confucius (551 BCE - 479 BCE) was a Chinese philosopher and educator. He believed in the importance of personal responsibility, respect for tradition, and the pursuit of knowledge. His philosophy centered around the Five Virtues: benevolence, righteousness, propriety, wisdom, and trustworthiness. He believed these virtues were essential for achieving a harmonious society and living a fulfilling life. His ideas have continued to shape Chinese culture and society, and his emphasis on education, ethics, and relationships continues to be relevant today.

Begin your day with this quote:

"Every day is a new beginning. Take a deep breath, smile, and start again."
Confucius

Remind yourself during the day:

"It does not matter how slowly you go as long as you do not stop."
Confucius

Read this quote and reflect at the end of the day:

"Wheresoever you go, go with all your heart."
Confucius

Lao Tzu (551 BCE - 479 BCE) was an ancient Chinese philosopher and poet. He is considered the founder of Taoism. Lao Tzu's philosophy centers around the concept of the Tao, which can be translated as "the way" or "the path". The Tao is characterized by simplicity, humility, and naturalness, and in his belief, these qualities should guide behavior and actions. He believed that the pursuit of wealth, power, and material possessions only leads to strife and suffering and that true happiness and fulfillment can only be found through inner peace and contentment.

Begin your day with this quote:

> *"Nature does not hurry, yet everything is accomplished."*
> Lao Tzu

Remind yourself during the day:

> *"The journey of a thousand miles begins with one step."*
> Lao Tzu

Read this quote and reflect at the end of the day:

> *"The best fighter is never angry."*
> Lao Tzu

Khwarizmi (780 -850 CE) was a Persian mathematician, astronomer, and scholar known as the father of algebra. His philosophy was heavily influenced by Islamic theology and mathematics. He believed that knowledge is essential for seeking truth and understanding the world around us. He also believed that balance and proportion are the foundation of the universe and that mathematics is the key to unlocking the mysteries of the natural world.

Begin your day with this quote:

"Knowledge is the companion of the seeker, the sharer in his/her loneliness, the guide to his/her journey, and the medicine to his/her ills."
Khwarizmi

Remind yourself during the day:

"Rest satisfied with doing well, and leave others to talk of you as they will."
Khwarizmi

Read this quote and reflect at the end of the day:

"The way to preserve the peace of the heart is to forgive and forget."
Khwarizmi

Farabi (870 - 950 CE) was a prominent Muslim philosopher, scientist, and musician who was born in Central Asia. He was greatly influenced by the works of Aristotle, which he translated into Arabic. His philosophy is characterized by the concept of the "Perfect State," in which the ruler was a philosopher-king who governed based on reason and justice. He believed that the ultimate goal of human life is to achieve happiness through the cultivation of virtue and the pursuit of knowledge. He also made significant contributions to the fields of mathematics, physics, and astronomy.

Begin your day with this quote:

"The first step towards wisdom is to recognize that you lack it."
Farabi

Remind yourself during the day:

"Productivity is achieved by working smart, not just working hard."
Farabi

Read this quote and reflect at the end of the day:

"The best way to end your day is with gratitude. Reflect on the good things that happened, and let go of the rest."
Farabi

Avicenna (980-1037 CE), also known as Ibn Sina, was a Persian polymath who made significant contributions to the fields of medicine, philosophy, and science. Avicenna's philosophy is based on the idea that reason and rational inquiry are essential for understanding the nature of the universe and our place in it. He believed that the universe is eternal and that all things, including human beings, are connected in a complex web of causality.

Begin your day with this quote:

"Rise early, and you will have a productive start to your day. The morning hours are precious; make the most of them."
Avicenna (Ibn Sina)

Remind yourself during the day:

"Happiness is the reward of a life lived according to virtue."
Avicenna (Ibn Sina)

Read this quote and reflect at the end of the day:

"The universe is a divine book, and the more we study it, the closer we come to the divine Author."
Avicenna (Ibn Sina)

Ghazali (1058 - 1111 CE) was a Persian Islamic theologian, philosopher, and mystic. His philosophy is based on the idea that true knowledge can only be obtained through direct experience and intuition, rather than through reason and logic alone. He believed that human beings have an innate capacity for spiritual intuition and that human's ultimate goal should be attaining knowledge of God through spiritual practice.

Begin your day with this quote:

"You possess a treasure within you that is infinitely greater than anything the world can offer."
Ghazali

Remind yourself during the day:

"The only limit to your realization of tomorrow will be your doubts of today."
Ghazali

Read this quote and reflect at the end of the day:

"Every breath you take is a step towards death, so make every breath count."
Ghazali

 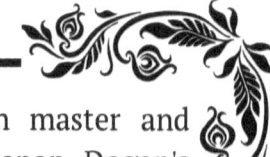

Dogen (1200 -1253 CE) was a Japanese Zen master and founder of the Soto, a Zen Buddhist school in Japan. Dogen's philosophy is rooted in the belief that enlightenment is not something to be attained through effort or striving but rather something that arises naturally from the present moment. He believed that the practice of zazen, or seated meditation, was the most direct path to realizing this truth.

Begin your day with this quote:

"Do not follow the ideas of others, but learn to listen to the voice within yourself. Your body and mind will become clear, and you will realize the unity of all things."
Dogen

Remind yourself during the day:

"When you are deluded and full of doubt, even a thousand books of scripture are not enough. When you have realized understanding, even one word is too much."
Dogen

Read this quote and reflect at the end of the day:

"Life and death are of supreme importance. Time swiftly passes by, and opportunity is lost. Each of us should strive to awaken. Awaken! Take heed, do not squander your life."
Dogen

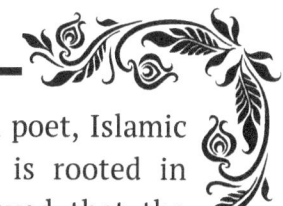

Jalaluddin Rumi (1207 -1273 CE) was a Persian poet, Islamic scholar, and Sufi mystic. Rumi's philosophy is rooted in Sufism, a mystical branch of Islam. He believed that the ultimate goal of human life is to achieve unity with God through love and devotion. Rumi's poetry often expresses this idea through vivid and emotional imagery, using love as a metaphor for the spiritual quest. Rumi's most famous work is the "Masnavi," a six-volume poem that explores themes of love, spirituality, and morality.

Begin your day with this quote:

"The breeze at dawn has secrets to tell you. Don't go back to sleep."
Rumi

Remind yourself during the day:

"Yesterday, I was clever, so I wanted to change the world. Today I am wise, so I am changing myself."
Rumi

Read this quote and reflect at the end of the day:

"You are not a drop in the ocean. You are the entire ocean in a drop."
Rumi

Hafiz (1315 -1390 CE) was a Persian poet and mystic who is widely regarded as one of the greatest poets in the Persian language. His philosophy is rooted in the Sufi tradition of Islamic mysticism and emphasizes the importance of love, joy, and spiritual union with the divine. He also emphasizes the importance of the inner life and the cultivation of spiritual awareness. He believed that the true path to enlightenment is not through formal religious practices or dogmatic beliefs but rather through a deep understanding of the self and a willingness to embrace the mysteries of existence.

Begin your day with this quote:

> *"I wish I could show you when you are lonely or in darkness, the astonishing light of your own being."*
> Hafiz

Remind yourself during the day:

> *"You carry all the ingredients to turn your existence into joy. Mix them, mix them!"*
> Hafiz

Read this quote and reflect at the end of the day:

> *"Let the beauty of what you love be what you do."*
> Hafiz

Ibn Khaldun (1332 -1406 CE) was a North African historian, philosopher, and sociologist known for his contributions to the field of social sciences. He is considered one of the most important thinkers in the history of Islamic scholarship. He believed that the study of history is essential for understanding human societies and their development over time. He believed that societies went through a cycle of growth and decline and that the decline was often caused by corruption and the loss of moral values.

Begin your day with this quote:

"Know that the true nature of wealth is to give, not to take."
Ibn Khaldun

Remind yourself during the day:

"He who has a thousand friends has not a friend to spare, and he who has one enemy will meet him everywhere."
Ibn Khaldun

Read this quote and reflect at the end of the day:

"Do not grieve over what has passed unless it makes you work harder for what is about to come."
Ibn Khaldun

Wang Yangming (1472-1529 CE) - Chinese philosopher and statesman known for his influential Neo-Confucian philosophy. His philosophy emphasized the importance of personal cultivation and self-reflection (the concept of "extension"-Tui, which he believed was the key to understanding the nature of reality). He believed that knowledge and action are inseparable and that one's understanding of the world must be rooted in direct experience rather than relying solely on traditional texts or inherited wisdom.

Begin your day with this quote:

"Every day is a new beginning. Every moment is a chance to change yourself for the better. Do not waste your time on things that do not matter."
Wang Yangming

Remind yourself during the day:

"To learn something and then put it into practice is useful. To know something but not put it into practice is of no use."
Wang Yangming

Read this quote and reflect at the end of the day:

"Do not regret what you have done. Do not be afraid to make mistakes. Learn from them and move on."
Wang Yangming

Matsuo Basho (1644 CE -1694 CE) was a Japanese poet of the Edo period and is considered one of the greatest masters of haiku poetry. Basho's philosophy is reflected in his poetry with two important Zen ideals, the concepts of "sabi" (which means "solitude") and "wabi" (which means "simplicity" and "humility"). His poetry often emphasizes the importance of simplicity, humility, and a deep connection to nature. He believed that poetry should capture the essence of a moment and convey a sense of the natural world's beauty and transience.

Begin your day with this quote:

"Every day is a journey, and the journey itself is home."
Matsuo Basho

Remind yourself during the day:

"Do not seek to follow in the footsteps of the wise. Seek what they sought."
Matsuo Basho

Read this quote and reflect at the end of the day:

"The past is already past. Don't try to regain it. The present is here. Grasp it firmly."
Matsuo Basho

Rabindranath Tagore (1861-1941 CE) was a Bengali-Indian poet, philosopher, musician, and polymath. He believed in the unity of humanity and sought to bridge the gap between Eastern and Western cultures. His philosophy emphasizes the importance of freedom, creativity, and individuality. He believed that true freedom could only be achieved through the pursuit of knowledge and understanding. He is known for his contributions to literature, music, and art, and his advocacy for Indian independence.

Begin your day with this quote:

"Every morning is a fresh beginning. Every day is the world made new. Today is a new day. Today is my world made new."
Rabindranath Tagore

Remind yourself during the day:

"The butterfly counts not months but moments, and has time enough."
Rabindranath Tagore

Read this quote and reflect at the end of the day:

"I have become my own version of an optimist. If I can't make it through one door, I'll go through another door - or I'll make a door. Something terrific will come no matter how dark the present."
Rabindranath Tagore

Byung-Chul Han is a contemporary South Korean-German philosopher, born in 1959. He is known for his critique of contemporary society, particularly the effects of digital technology and neoliberal capitalism on the human psyche. His philosophy emphasizes the need for a new form of critical thinking. One of Han's key contributions to philosophy is his concept of "psycho-politics," which refers to how power is exercised through the manipulation of the individual psyche. He argues that digital technology and social media have created a form of constant surveillance and self-monitoring, leading to a loss of privacy and individuality. This, in turn, leads to a form of self-exploitation and exhaustion, which he terms "neurasthenia."

Begin your day with this quote:

"Every morning is a chance to live a new life. Don't let yesterday's problems weigh you down."
Byung-Chul Han

Remind yourself during the day:

"Instead of trying to do everything, focus on doing a few things really well. Quality over quantity."
Byung-Chul Han

Read this quote and reflect at the end of the day:

"Don't forget to take a break and rest. It's not laziness, it's self-care. You deserve it."
Byung-Chul Han

Quotes from Western Philosophers and Scholars

Socrates (469/470 – 399 BCE) was a Greek philosopher from Athens and is known for his Socratic method of questioning, which involved asking a series of questions to uncover the truth or knowledge. He believed that true knowledge is innate and can be brought forth through inquiry. Socrates' philosophy examines how we should live. He believed that people should care less about their bodies and possessions and more about their soul.

Begin your day with this quote:

"The only true wisdom is in knowing you know nothing."
Socrates

Remind yourself during the day:

"An unexamined life is not worth living."
Socrates

Read this quote and reflect at the end of the day:

"Be as you wish to seem."
Socrates

Plato (428/427 BCE – 348/347 BCE) was a student of Socrates and the founder of the Academy in Athens. His philosophy is focused on the idea of Forms, which he believed were perfect, abstract concepts that exist outside of the physical world. These Forms are the essences of various objects. He believed every object or quality in this world has an ideal form that is timeless and unchanging, and every object in the physical world was a mere shadow mimicking the Form.

Begin your day with this quote:

"The first and greatest victory is to conquer yourself."
Plato

Remind yourself during the day:

"The heaviest penalty for declining to rule is to be ruled by someone inferior to yourself."
Plato

Read this quote and reflect at the end of the day:

"We can easily forgive a child who is afraid of the dark; the real tragedy of life is when men are afraid of the light."
Plato

Aristotle (384 BCE – 322 BCE) was a Greek philosopher and a student of Plato and a renowned polymath. His philosophy focused on the idea of causation and the study of nature. He believed that everything has a purpose and function, and that knowledge is obtained through experience and observation.

Begin your day with this quote:

"It is during our darkest moments that we must focus to see the light."
Aristotle

Remind yourself during the day:

"Pleasure in the job puts perfection in the work."
Aristotle

Read this quote and reflect at the end of the day:

"The roots of education are bitter, but the fruit is sweet."
Aristotle

Boethius (480 - 524) was a Roman philosopher who wrote on a variety of topics, including music, logic, and theology. His most famous work is "The Consolation of Philosophy," which he wrote while imprisoned awaiting execution. The book is a dialogue between Boethius and Lady Philosophy, in which she consoles him and explains the nature of happiness, free will, and the nature of God.

Begin your day with this quote:

> *"The beginning of all things is small."*
> Boethius

Remind yourself during the day:

> *"True happiness is not derived from external possessions; it comes from within the soul."*
> Boethius

Read this quote and reflect at the end of the day:

> *"As the sun went down, I saw a little flower standing alone in a field. It had no companion of its own kind, and so it was crying for company. But its cries went unheard. It was destined to live its life alone. So it lifted its head gracefully and decided to dance in the gentle breeze that had begun to blow. And in its dance, it found joy that no companion could have ever given it."*
> Boethius

William Shakespeare (1564 - 1616) was an English playwright and poet who is widely considered one of the greatest writers in the English language. His philosophy often explores universal themes such as love, death, and human nature. He believed that the purpose of art was to hold a mirror up to nature, and his plays often examine the complexities of human relationships and the consequences of our actions.

Begin your day with this quote:

"All the world's a stage, and all the men and women merely players."
Shakespeare

Remind yourself during the day:

"We know what we are but know not what we may be."
Shakespeare

Read this quote and reflect at the end of the day:

"All things are ready if our minds be so."
Shakespeare

René Descartes (1596 – 1650) was a French mathematician, a natural scientist or "natural philosopher", and a metaphysician. He is known for his skepticism and his belief in the separation of mind and body. He famously said, "I think, therefore I am," which became a cornerstone of Western philosophy.

Begin your day with this quote:

"The reading of all good books is like a conversation with the finest minds of past centuries."
René Descartes

Remind yourself during the day:

"Divide each difficulty into as many parts as is feasible and necessary to resolve it."
René Descartes

Read this quote and reflect at the end of the day:

"Each problem that I solved became a rule which served afterward to solve other problems."
René Descartes

Sir Isaac Newton (1643 - 1727) was an English physicist and mathematician who is widely considered one of the most influential scientists in history. Newton's philosophy emphasized the power of reason and observation in understanding the natural world. He believed the universe was an ordered system that could be described and understood through mathematical principles.

Begin your day with this quote:

"This most beautiful system of the sun, planets, and comets could only proceed from the counsel and dominion of an intelligent and powerful Being."
Isaac Newton

Remind yourself during the day:

"We build too many walls and not enough bridges."
Isaac Newton

Read this quote and reflect at the end of the day:

"I do not know what I may appear to the world, but to myself, I seem to have been only like a boy playing on the seashore, and diverting myself in now and then finding a smoother pebble or a prettier shell than ordinary, whilst the great ocean of truth lay all undiscovered before me."
Isaac Newton

George Berkeley (1685 to 1753) was an Irish philosopher who is known for his philosophy of immaterialism, which suggests that the physical world only exists as it is perceived by the mind. According to Berkeley, objects do not exist independently of the mind, and all sensory experiences are dependent on the observer's perception. His philosophy emphasized the importance of perception and experience in shaping our understanding of reality, and he believed that the world was fundamentally made up of ideas rather than physical matter.

Begin your day with this quote:

"Every man has a right to be valued by his best moments."
George Berkeley

Remind yourself during the day:

"The world is like a mirror; frown at it, and it frowns at you. Smile, and it smiles too."
George Berkeley

Read this quote and reflect at the end of the day:

"All the choir of heaven and furniture of earth, in a word all those bodies which compose the mighty frame of the world, have not any subsistence without a mind."
George Berkeley

Jean-Jacques Rousseau (1712 - 1778) was a Swiss-French philosopher, writer, and composer who is best known for his contributions to political philosophy and his influence on the French Revolution. His philosophy was grounded in his belief in the fundamental goodness of human beings and the corrupting influence of civilization. He argued that human beings were naturally free and equal but that society and its institutions had created inequality and injustice.

Begin your day with this quote:

"The world of reality has its limits; the world of imagination is boundless."
Jean-Jacques Rousseau

Remind yourself during the day:

"Freedom is not worth having if it does not include the freedom to make mistakes."
Jean-Jacques Rousseau

Read this quote and reflect at the end of the day:

"The greatest glory in living lies not in never falling, but in rising every time we fall."
Jean-Jacques Rousseau

Immanuel Kant (1724 – 1804) was a German philosopher who is known for his moral and ethical philosophy. His moral philosophy is known as philosophy of freedom. He believed without human freedom, moral appraisal and moral responsibility would be impossible. He believed that moral principles are grounded in reason and that individuals have a duty to act in accordance with these principles.

Begin your day with this quote:

"The greatest happiness principle holds that the ultimate end, the supreme good, is an existence exempt from pain and rich in enjoyments."
Immanuel Kant

Remind yourself during the day:

"Science is organized knowledge. Wisdom is organized life."
Immanuel Kant

Read this quote and reflect at the end of the day:

"Live your life as though your every act were to become a universal law."
Immanuel Kant

 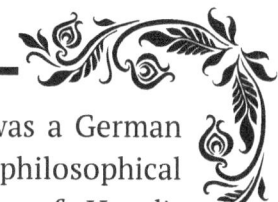

Georg Wilhelm Friedrich Hegel (1770 -1831) was a German philosopher who developed a comprehensive philosophical system known as Hegelianism. At the core of Hegel's philosophy was the idea of dialectic, a process of thesis, antithesis, and synthesis that he believed could be applied to all aspects of human thought and history.

Begin your day with this quote:

> *"Nothing great in the world has ever been accomplished without passion."*
> Hegel

Remind yourself during the day:

"Life has value only when it has something valuable as its object."
Hegel

Read this quote and reflect at the end of the day:

"The history of the world is none other than the progress of the consciousness of freedom."
Hegel

Friedrich Nietzsche (1844 – 1900) was a German philosopher who rejected traditional values and beliefs and instead focused on the concept of individualism and the will to power. He believed the meaning of life comes from our choice and it is not something to be dictated by society or religion. He is also known for his critique of Christianity and the idea of God being dead.

Begin your day with this quote:

"He who has a why to live for can bear almost any how."
Friedrich Nietzsche

Remind yourself during the day:

"The greatest happiness is to know the source of unhappiness."
Friedrich Nietzsche

Read this quote and reflect at the end of the day:

"To live is to suffer, to survive is to find some meaning in the suffering."
Friedrich Nietzsche

Albert Einstein (1879 - 1955) was a German theoretical physicist and philosopher who is widely considered one of the most influential scientists of the 20th century. He is best known for developing the theory of relativity. Einstein's philosophy was rooted in his belief that the universe is governed by a set of fundamental laws and that these laws can be discovered through empirical observation and mathematical reasoning.

Begin your day with this quote:

"Learn from yesterday, live for today, hope for tomorrow. The important thing is not to stop questioning."
Albert Einstein

Remind yourself during the day:

"Logic will get you from A to B. Imagination will take you everywhere."
Albert Einstein

Read this quote and reflect at the end of the day:

"Try not to become a person of success, but rather try to become a person of value."
Albert Einstein

Jean-Paul Sartre (1905 – 1980) was a French philosopher who is associated with existentialism. He believed that individuals are free to make their own choices and that there is no inherent meaning in the world. He famously wrote, "Existence precedes essence." He argued that the realization of our freedom and the inherent meaninglessness of existence can lead to feelings of anxiety, despair, and meaninglessness. He believed that we must confront these feelings and find our meaning and purpose in life.

Begin your day with this quote:

"Life begins on the other side of despair."
Jean-Paul Sartre

Remind yourself during the day:

"We are our choices."
Jean-Paul Sartre

Read this quote and reflect at the end of the day:

"In the end, we only regret the chances we didn't take."
Jean-Paul Sartre

Quentin Meillassoux is a contemporary French philosopher who was born in 1967. He is associated with the speculative realism movement and is known for his work on metaphysics, ontology, and epistemology. He critiques the Kantian notion that we can only know the world as it appears to us, arguing instead that we can know the world in itself, independently of our subjective experience.

Begin your day with this quote:

"Wake up with a sense of wonder and curiosity about the world around you. Embrace the mystery of existence and strive to understand the nature of reality."
Quentin Meillassoux

Remind yourself during the day:

"In the face of uncertainty and chaos, don't be afraid to seek out new knowledge and ideas. The pursuit of truth and understanding is a noble goal."
Quentin Meillassoux

Read this quote and reflect at the end of the day:

"Take time to reflect on the events of your day and consider the ways in which you have grown and changed. Every experience is an opportunity to learn and develop as a person."
Quentin Meillassoux

The Power of Your Thoughts

You are your thoughts, coming in tones,
The rest's nothing but flesh and bones,
Your mind's the music of your life,
So choose your thoughts with care and thrive.

Your thoughts are like a symphony,
Creating your reality,
Positive tones can lift you high,
Negative ones can make you sigh.

Your mind is like a painter's brush,
A place where tones can mix and rush,
Choose them wisely, let go of the rest,
And let your inner joy be expressed.

You are your thoughts, coming in tones,
A language's spoken deep within your bones,
So take control of your inner voice,
And watch your life becomes your choice.

You are your thoughts, coming in tones,
The rest's nothing but flesh and bones,
So play your mind like a beautiful song,
And let your heart sings with you along.

www.ingramcontent.com/pod-product-compliance
Lightning Source LLC
Chambersburg PA
CBHW021126080526
44587CB00010B/649